Four Sides, Eight Nights

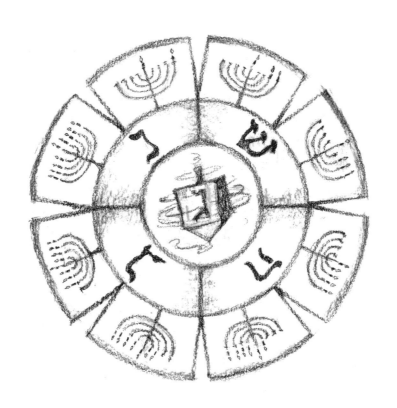

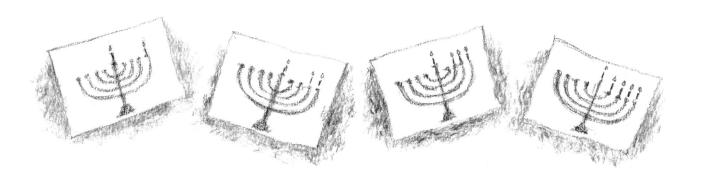

Four Sides, Eight Nights
A New Spin on Hanukkah

By Rebecca Tova Ben-Zvi
Illustrated by Susanna Natti

A Deborah Brodie Book
Roaring Brook Press
New Milford, Connecticut

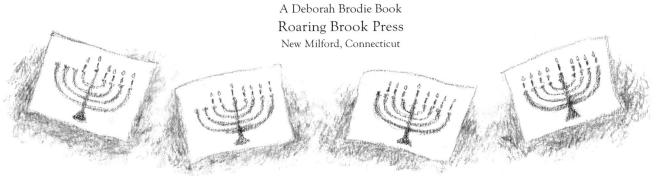

Text copyright © 2005 by Rebecca Tova Ben-Zvi

Illustrations copyright © 2005 by Susanna Natti

A Deborah Brodie Book

Published by Roaring Brook Press

Roaring Brook Press is a division of Holtzbrinck Publishing Holdings Limited Partnership

143 West Street, New Milford, Connecticut 06776

Distributed In Canada by H. B. Fenn and Company Ltd.

Library of Congress Cataloging-in-Publication Data

Ben-Zvi, Rebecca Tova.

Four sides, eight nights : a new spin on Hanukkah / by Rebecca Tova Ben-Zvi ; illustrated by Susanna Natti.— 1st ed.

p. cm.

"A Deborah Brodie book."

ISBN-10: 1-59643-059-1   ISBN-13: 978-1-59643-059-4 (hardcover)

ISBN-10: 1-59643-181-4   ISBN-13: 978-1-59643-181-2 (paperback)

1. Hanukkah—Juvenile literature.   I. Natti, Susanna. II. Title.

BM695.H3B466 2005

296.4′35—dc22

2004022562

Roaring Brook Press books are available for special promotions and premiums.

For details contact: Director of Special Markets, Holtzbrinck Publishers.

First edition September 2005

First paperback edition October 2006

Book design by Jennifer Browne

Printed in the United States of America

2   4   6   8   10   9   7   5   3 (hardcover)   2   4   6   8   10   9   7   5   3   1 (paperback)

To my parents, Paul and Linda Ben-Zvi. You're the tops!

—R.T. B.-Z.

Remembering with love "the hubbub of the universe,"
my mother-in-law,
Beatrice Willsky
S. N.

Contents

The best thing about Hanukkah is the presents!
I gave my parents a papier-mâché city I made at school.
They put it up on the mantel.

My favorite part is playing
dreidel. We have a big game with all the grandkids
and cousins and uncles and aunts. Last year,
my dog even played with us. (I spun for
him, though.)

Well, my favorite part is the latkes!
My brother and I help grate the potatoes.
We serve them with sour cream and home-
made applesauce. They are sooo good!

I like lighting the Hanukkah menorah,
the *hanukkiyah*. My sister and I each have
our own. After we light the candles and say
the blessing, we listen to Mom and Dad tell
us the story of Hanukkah.

CHAPTER 1

How Hanukkah Happened

No Judaism. That was the law. No Jewish weddings. No Sabbath prayers. No special celebrations at the birth of a baby. No Torah study in the Temple. No Jewish anything. In 168 B.C.E., Syrian-Greek king Antiochus IV (An-TIE-uh-cuss) outlawed the Jewish religion. Anyone caught practicing Judaism was put to death.

What's the Difference?

Q: *The menorah in the ancient Temple of Judea had seven branches. The Hanukkah menorah we light today has nine. What's the difference?*
A: *Two!*
Actually, the ancient menorah was a six-foot-high, richly decorated oil lamp of pure gold. Each of its seven branches was topped with a cup in the shape of an almond blossom. Every evening, the oil in the cups was lit, and the light of the menorah illuminated the Temple until morning.
The hanukkiyah, *the Hanukkah menorah, can be almost any size or shape. It can hold candles or cups of oil, but it always has room for nine lights. Eight lights stand for the eight nights of Hanukkah, and the ninth light is the* shammash, *the helper candle used to light the others.*

But the Jewish people held on to their beliefs. They married on the sly. They welcomed the Sabbath in private. They quietly blessed their newborn babies. And in small groups, in alleyways and courtyards throughout Jerusalem, they continued to study Torah. If the Syrian-Greek soldiers caught them, the story goes, the students brought out a little top and gave it a spin. "We're not studying; we're playing. See?" Gambling was legal; the top saved their lives.

In the wild, rocky hills outside Jerusalem, Judah Maccabee led his people in a fight for religious freedom. Antiochus's soldiers were well trained, well fed, and well armed. The Maccabees were not. Yet they won many battles.

If I Had a Maccabee

Maccabee means "hammer." Judah earned the nickname by pounding his foes. Lee Hays and Pete Seeger probably weren't thinking about the Maccabees when they wrote "The Hammer Song," some 2,100 years later, but the song is curiously appropriate for Hanukkah. The song says that we already have the tools we need to win justice, freedom, and love. For half a century, it has been a call to political action and the unofficial anthem of the few struggling for freedom against the many. The Maccabees would have loved it!

They won back their Temple. The Syrian-Greeks had taken it over. It was not fit for a place of Jewish worship. The Maccabees restored it, and had a ceremony to rededicate it.

One of the Temple's great treasures had been the menorah, a gold oil lamp with seven branches. When the Maccabees returned to the Temple, the original lamp was gone. They made a new one and prepared to light it. The menorah burned a special, pure oil, but only one small bottle of oil could be found.

The King's Nickname

*Antiochus IV called himself Antiochus Epiphanes. Epiphanes means "like a god," but his subjects gave him a nickname, too. They changed the **ph** to **m** and called him Antiochus Epimanes—"the Madman."*

The Jews poured the oil into the lamp. They lit the flame, and the oil burned. It was such a small amount of oil, it should have run out after one night. Tradition tells us, though, that it burned on and on. It lasted throughout the rededication celebration: eight nights.

At Hanukkah, we remember that long-ago victory for religious freedom and the miracle of the oil. We celebrate with songs, gifts, and festive meals. And we play with a toy like the one that may have saved the Torah students in the time of the Maccabees: the dreidel.

The Dreidel Code

נ   *nun—Do nothing*

ג   *gimmel—Take all*

ה   *hay—Take half*

ש   *shin—Put one in*

CHAPTER 2

The Dreidel Family Tree

The Jews of ancient Judea spun a top to cover their forbidden Torah study, but it probably did not look like the dreidel we play with today. Today's dreidel is a four-sided spinning top with a letter on each of its sides. It's like a cross between a top and a die. This many-sided top has ancient origins. The dreidel as we know it developed from sheep bones and fire starters.

Tali, or knucklebones, are rectangular bones from the feet of sheep, and they were very popular as dice at the time of Judah Maccabee. There were even imitation tali made of metal. The ancient Greeks called them *astragali* and invented complex games for them.

Astragali had four sides and no pips. The shape of the bone determined each side's value. Modern dice are rolled by hand or thrown from a cup, but astragali were cast by spinning them. A spinning, four-sided die? That's the world's earliest dreidel.

But a dreidel is a top, and tops go back a long way. Early humans developed the top from the fire drill—not the fire drill where your class spends some time outdoors as a safety exercise; the fire drill that ancient people used to start a fire.

A fire drill is a slender bit, spun upright on a base. If it spins fast enough, it can start a fire. You might say the earliest top was not a toy. It was an instrument of survival.

Toy tops are as old as

Teetotums the World Around (and around and around . . .)

Rokuhaku is a Japanese top with six sides. Instead of letters, each side has a different pattern of shapes.

French board games of the eighteenth century used many-sided tops to assign playing pieces or to count the number of spaces a player could move.

A five-sided spinning top was used instead of dice in a nineteenth-century Korean board game called tiyong-kyeng-toe. The top had notches instead of letters.

history and as widespread as civilization. Archaeologists have found antique tops from Alaska to Malaysia to King Tut's tomb. The dreidel has cousins throughout history and all over the world.

A popular game in ancient Rome used a four-sided spinning top with a letter on each of its sides: *T* for *totum*, the Latin word for "all"; *A* for *aufer*, Latin for "take away"; *D* for *depone*, meaning "put"; and *N* for *nihil*, "nothing." Sound familiar?

Roman culture had spread throughout Europe, and by the Middle Ages, the little top had traveled far and wide. Wherever it went, it was a wintertime favorite because it could be played indoors. In

Foot-Bone Fortunes

Knucklebones were used for telling fortunes in ancient Rome. Each bone had a flat side, a wavy side, a side that curved out, and a side that curved in. Several tali were thrown at once. If four flat sides landed upward, it was said to be bad luck.

concave

convex

flat

sinuous

England it was called a *teetotum. Tee* meant the letter *T*; *totum* meant "all." When the top landed on *T*, the spinner took all—teetotum.

European Jews spoke Yiddish, and they called the top *dreidel. Drehen* is the Yiddish word for "turn." Their dreidel had Hebrew letters on its sides (Yiddish uses the Hebrew alphabet): *Nun* for *nisht*, the Yiddish word for "nothing"; *gimmel* for *gahntz*, Yiddish for "all"; *hay* for *halb*, meaning "half"; *shin* for *shtel*, "put."

Happily, these letters—*gimmel, hay, shin,* and *nun*—were also the first letters in the words *Nes gadol hayah sham:* "A great miracle happened there." The dreidel wasn't just a toy top. It was a game to help everyone remember the Hanukkah miracle. And it still is.

CHAPTER 3

Nun, Gimmel, Hay, Shin

Advice on Gaming

"You ought to play in such a way that it does not matter how the dice fall, as will be the case if you play for small stakes or with your loved ones for a short time after dinner."

    —Gerolamo Cardano, Sixteenth-century mathematical genius and gambling expert

How to Play

At our house, we use chocolate chip cookies. Everybody gets ten. We each put one in the center of the table before the first spin. That's the pot. We put more in the pot if it's empty; for instance, after someone gets a *gimmel*. We take turns using a big wooden dreidel. Whoever has the most cookies at the end of an hour, wins. Once, my brother ended up with sixty cookies!

Po in Israel

Israeli dreidels don't have the letter shin. Instead, they have the letter pey, for po, the Hebrew word for "here." In Israel, the dreidels remind us, "a great miracle happened here."

In our family, we play with buttons. My grandma has a big jarful. She lets my cousins and me each pick out twelve to play with. I try to find all blues. Grandma tells us to "ante up," and we each put a button in the middle of the table. Grandma calls that the "kitty." We add to the kitty after each turn, so it never runs out. The game is over when one player has all the buttons. It's usually Grandma.

Before Hanukkah, we look for pennies all over the house—under couch cushions, in the junk drawer, at the bottom of our gym bags, and, of course, in our piggy banks. We use whatever we find to play dreidel. At the end of the game, we wrap up all the pennies in rolls and give them to the food bank.

Sevivon

The Hebrew word for "dreidel" is sevivon, from the root word sabov, "to spin around."

Our Hebrew school teacher gives each of us our own plastic dreidel. We play for points. In Hebrew, each letter has a number. *Nun* is 50. *Gimmel* is 3. *Hay* is 5 and *shin* is 300. Whoever gets the most points, wins. It's the only time I'm happy to get *shin*! After that, we have a spinning contest. We all spin our dreidels at the same time. The one whose dreidel spins the longest, wins.

dirndl—a style of skirt that poofs out when its wearer spins like a dreidel.

treadle—a pedal that, when pressed, makes a wheel on a machine spin like a dreidel!

Top (ha-ha, get it?) Eight Betting Units for Playing Dreidel

8. Raisins—according to one legend, Judith brought dried fruit to Holophernes. [hollow-FAIR-knees] (More on Judith in Chapter 6, "A Holiday Within a Holiday.")

7. Animal crackers—especially elephants, for the armored beasts the Syrian-Greeks used in battle, and lions, the symbol of Judah Maccabee.

6. Macadamias—kinda sounds like "Maccabees." Besides, the macademia's natural nut-oil reminds us of the Hanukkah miracle.

5. Chocolate Kisses—kinda sounds like "Kislev," the Hebrew month in which Hanukkah occurs.

4. Pebbles—in honor of the rocky terrain where the Maccabees hid.

3. Almonds—a crop of ancient Judea (not to mention: a good source of calcium, magnesium, and zinc).

2. Chocolate *gelt*—a popular treat. Eat the chocolate, and save the foil to make your own miniature hanukkiyah.

1. Coins—students traditionally collected Hanukkah *gelt* (money) to pay their teachers. Giving dreidel winnings to charity is another Hanukkah tradition.

CHAPTER 4

I Have a Little Dreidel

"My Dreidel"

I have a little dreidel,
I made it out of clay.
And when it's dry and ready
Then dreidel I shall play.

O dreidel, dreidel, dreidel,
I made it out of clay.
O dreidel, dreidel, dreidel,
Now dreidel I shall play.

It has a lovely body,
With leg so short and thin.
And when it is all tired,
It drops and then I win.

O dreidel, dreidel, dreidel,
With leg so short and thin.
O dreidel, dreidel, dreidel,
It drops and then I win.

My dreidel is always playful,
It loves to dance and spin.
A happy game of dreidel,
Come play, now let's begin.

O dreidel, dreidel, dreidel,
It loves to dance and spin.
O dreidel, dreidel, dreidel,
Come play, now let's begin.

Before Talkies

Samuel Goldfarb supplemented his Bureau of Jewish Education income by playing the Wurlitzer—a giant pipe organ—in a theater for silent movies.

My Dad Wrote "My Dreidel"

Samuel Goldfarb had five children: one daughter and four sons.

"My Dreidel" may be the most well-known Hanukkah song in America. It was written by Samuel Grossman and Samuel Eliezer Goldfarb. The words are by Samuel Grossman. Samuel Goldfarb wrote the music.

Samuel Goldfarb was the fourth of eleven children. His family came to the United States around the turn of the twentieth century, when Samuel was a child. He grew up in Brooklyn, New York, and became the first music director for the Bureau of Jewish Education in New York City. He worked there until 1929. He led singing groups for grown-ups and taught children folksongs in Hebrew and Yiddish. He wrote music, too: hymns, prayers, school songs. With his collaborator, Samuel Grossman, he even wrote an opera! But their most famous song is "My Dreidel."

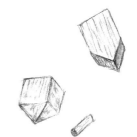

CHAPTER 5

I Made It Out Of . . .

Wood

One thousand pounds of wood went into the giant Dreidel House in New Brunswick, New Jersey.

Michael Moshe Verter designed the Dreidel House for the Chabad Jewish student organization at Rutgers University. It is eight feet wide and eighteen feet tall. The carved wooden letters on its sides are five feet tall. That's taller than most sixth graders!

The giant dreidel doesn't spin, but it does have front and back doors so that people can go inside it. It can hold more than fifty people at a time!

Molten Lead

In the early twentieth century, children in Eastern Europe used to make their own dreidels out of hot, liquid lead. They made the molds out of wood. They had to carve the Hebrew letters in reverse so that they would look right on the finished dreidel. Then they poured in the hot metal from a spoon. Don't try this at home!

wooden mold piece

wooden mold pieces bundled and ready for pouring

funnel piece

poured lead dreidel

cut off funnel for finished dreidel

Silver, Gold, Gemstones, Porcelain, or Glass

Dreidels can be fine art. Museums, galleries, and private collectors have lovingly crafted, perfectly balanced dreidels in an endless variety of designs. Rabbi Sara Perman of Greensburg, Pennsylvania, has been collecting dreidels since she was a little girl. Now she has more than 400. One of her dreidels is made of brass and unfolds to become a Hanukkah menorah. She has another in the shape of a ballet dancer. She has dreidels made of antique glass and sterling silver and a dreidel made of chocolate.

She says collecting dreidels is fun: "They're toys. You can play with them." A dreidel is also a reminder of the Hanukkah miracle. A beautiful dreidel, created with care, polished and cherished, honors the Hanukkah miracle.

How Do You Start Your Day?

In the civil calendar, a new day begins at midnight, but in the Hebrew calendar, sunset is the start of a new day. A full day is from sunset to sunset. When Jewish holidays are recorded on the civil calendar, it looks like Jewish holidays start the night before.

CHAPTER 6

A Holiday Within a Holiday

Rosh Hodesh (rosh HO-desh) is the first day of a new month in the Hebrew calendar. It is the day when the first sliver of the new moon appears in the sky. Hanukkah starts on the twenty-fifth of the Hebrew month of *Kislev*, so *Rosh Hodesh Tevet*, the first night of the month of *Tevet*, is the sixth night of Hanukkah. It is traditionally a time to remember the heroines of Hanukkah.

The Legend of Judith: Say "Cheese"

The people of Bethulia had to choose: surrender to the Syrian-Greeks or die of thirst. Antiochus had sent his most powerful general, Holophernes (hollow-FAIR-knees), to destroy the city. His army surrounded Bethulia and cut off the water supply, but a rich, beautiful widow named Judith had a plan.

Judith got dressed up; packed some fruit, bread, and cheese in a bag; and, with her maidservant, walked out to meet Holophernes. If the Syrian-Greek soldiers thought it strange that two enemy women should come waltzing into their army camp, Judith soon laid their suspicions to rest. She explained that she had left the city because

Elazar

Elazar (el-ah-ZAR) was the brother of Judah Maccabee and the husband of Hannah (see page 34). He died a hero. The Maccabees fought on foot, with simple weapons. The Syrian-Greeks fought with powerful weapons, on elephants!

When the Maccabees saw the Syrian-Greeks riding up on armored elephants, they lost heart. Elazar knew what to do. He ran to the lead elephant and stood beneath its chest. Stabbing his spear straight up, he killed the beast. The elephant fell, crushing Elazar, but the Maccabees had seen his deed. Inspired by Elazar's bravery, they fought hard and won the battle.

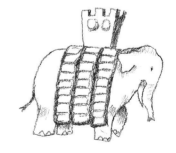

she was sure the Syrian-Greeks would conquer it any day now, and she'd like to help them. Holophernes was flattered. He asked Judith to stay and be his guest.

She accepted, with a few conditions. She and her maidservant would eat only the food they had brought with them. (It was **kosher**, specially prepared according to Jewish law.) They would also leave the camp each day before dawn to pray by themselves, returning after their prayers.

They stayed for four days. All Holophernes could talk about was how wise and beautiful Judith was. He threw her a party in his tent, but he invited only one guest: Judith.

In keeping with their agreement, Judith brought her own food. She shared it with Holophernes. She fed him cheese—salty cheese— cheese that was so salty, Holophernes became very, very thirsty. "More wine?" offered Judith, and poured him glass after glass.

That night, Holophernes drank more wine than he had ever drunk before. It made him so sleepy, he finally stretched out, unconscious, on his bed.

The general kept his sword hanging on his bedpost. Judith took it down. With one hand on the sword and the other in Holophernes' long hair, Judith whacked him on the neck, rolled his body onto the floor, and handed his severed head to her maid.

A little while later, Judith and her maidservant strolled out of the camp. If any of the soldiers noticed them—and the big bag the maidservant was carrying— they just assumed the women were going out to pray, as usual, and left them alone.

When the Syrian-Greek soldiers discovered their headless leader, they turned and ran in a panicked mob.

The story of Judith's bravery traveled fast. Not only did Judith save Bethulia, but her example renewed her people's resolve to defeat Antiochus.

On Hanukkah, we eat a meal with cheese, sour cream, or other dairy foods in memory of the salty cheese Judith gave Holophernes long ago.

Two Hannahs, Two Heroines

At Hanukkah, we recount the legends of two different women named Hannah: Hannah the Bride and Hannah the Mother. Each, in her own way, bravely defied the evil King Antiochus.

Hannah the Bride turned her wedding into a rally for freedom. At her marriage to Elazar—Judah Maccabee's brother—Hannah stood up in front of all the guests and tore off her clothes. Everyone was scandalized! "Get dressed! What are you doing?"

"I am making a point. If you're shocked to see me naked, then you should be even more shocked by Antiochus's cruel laws. They require much worse."

"But you have nothing on! Cut it out! You're embarrassing us!"

"I'm not embarrassing you. Antiochus is destroying our traditions. That is what embarrasses you. He thinks his outrageous laws can make us forget our religion. If you prove him right, if you don't overthrow his tyranny, then you have much more to be ashamed of than seeing a naked woman."

She convinced them. The Maccabees went directly from the wedding to the soldiers' headquarters and won their first battle in the war for religious freedom.

Hannah the Mother won a different kind of battle, a battle of wills. This Hannah had seven sons. Antiochus himself commanded them to give up Judaism. All seven refused. They paid with their lives, but their example strengthened the Jewish people's resistance.

The Sevivon in Space

In 1993, Astronaut Dr. Jeffrey Hoffman was aboard the space shuttle Endeavour during Hanukkah, but he still played dreidel. He brought a dreidel with him and spun it in zero gravity.

CHAPTER 7

Sevivon Science

Will I Win? What Are the Odds?

'Round and 'round and 'round it goes. Where it stops, nobody knows! That's because the game of dreidel is based on the science of probability.

Q: Suppose you and your friends are playing a game of dreidel. Six of you are sharing one dreidel, and you're still waiting for your

first turn. So far, everyone else has gotten *shin*. Assuming you're using a good, well-balanced dreidel, what are the chances that you'll get *gimmel*?

A: One in four. You have a 25 % chance of getting *gimmel*—or any other letter on the top. On a fair dreidel, each side has an equal chance of landing face-up at the end of a spin, even if it's been *shin* five times in a row.

If Sir Isaac had had a dreidel......

I wonder if this teetotum could spin forever?

The Sevivon of Sir Isaac Newton

When a dreidel—or any kind of top—spins so fast in one place that it looks like it isn't even moving, it is called going to sleep. When it stops spinning and falls over, it's said to be dead.

It's OK - I'm just playing dead

Sir Isaac Newton (1642–1727) was an English physicist. His discoveries shaped the way we understand our world. He researched the law of gravity and the motions of the stars. His science is also useful for explaining the dynamics of a dreidel. Newton's first law of motion states: "A body in motion tends to stay in motion." This is called the **law of inertia**.

According to the law of inertia, a spinning dreidel will keep spinning unless something makes it stop. But how can that be true? We see dreidels stop by themselves all the time. Here's what's going on. The dreidel is stopped by **friction**.

Friction happens when two surfaces touch. When a dreidel spins, the base of the dreidel rubs against the tabletop. The sides and top of the dreidel drag through the air. This slows down the dreidel.

Michael Berkowicz is a physicist today. He and designer Bonnie Srolovitz used scientific principles to design the Space Age Dreidel. Its shape allows it to spin faster and longer than a typical dreidel spins. The secrets are low friction and a low center of gravity.

Its spherical base lets the Space Age Dreidel spin on a **tangential point**. That means less of the dreidel's surface touches the table. And *that* means less friction and a longer spinning time. The round base also means the Space Age Dreidel weighs more toward its base than its stem—it has a low center of gravity. The low center of gravity lets the Space Age Dreidel tip less as it spins, so its sides avoid friction with the table for a longer time, and it spins longer than a typical dreidel.

A gold-and-brass Space Age Dreidel is in The Jewish Museum in New York City, but you don't need a Space Age Dreidel to get a good spin. When choosing a dreidel or making one of your own, remember: the ones with low friction and a low center of gravity are the best spinners.

Sevivon Speed

Q: With how much speed can a sevivon spin, when a sevivon spins with speed?

A: About 3,300 rpm (revolutions per minute)!

(A music CD spins at about 500 rpm.)

Are you sure it's 3,300 rpm? That's pretty fast!

Sure, I'm sure. Douglas W. Gould, an engineer who loves spinning tops, used a stroboscope to figure it out.

A stroboscope?

It's a machine with an adjustable quickly-flashing light. When the light flashes at the same rate as a rotating object, the object appears to stand still.

I've seen strobe lights at the science museum.

It's like that. Anyway, D. W. Gould measured the rotation speed of several kinds of tops. A plastic twirler, like a dreidel, spun between 3,200 and 3,400 rpm.

CHAPTER 8

Goodies and *Gelt*

Hannukah by the Numbers

Number of days' worth of oil the Maccabees found in the Temple: **1**

Number of days it lasted: **8**

Number of candles it takes to celebrate Hanukkah, if you burn one plus the shammash on the first night and add one more each night for the next seven nights: **44**

The menorah burns most brightly on the eighth night of Hanukkah, when all the candles are lit. It is a night for giving gifts and enjoying special foods.

Foods fried in oil are a Hanukkah tradition. The cooking oil reminds us of the Hanukkah miracle. Jelly doughnuts called *sufganiyot* are an Israeli Hanukkah treat. Latkes—pancakes fried in oil—are popular in the United States. They are usually made of grated white potatoes and are served with applesauce and sour cream, but they don't have to be. You can try all kinds of delicious ingredients in your latkes.

Substitute the potatoes in your latke recipe with this

Serve them with this

chopped apples and walnuts

cinnamon and sugar

cottage cheese

strawberry jam

peanut butter

grape jelly

crushed pineapple

shredded coconut

cooked, mashed pinto beans

salsa

cooked, pureed pumpkin

nutmeg and powdered sugar

grated sweet potatoes

sour cream

grated zucchini

marinara sauce and parmesan cheese

Eight Hanukkah Dos and Don'ts

1. Do put your menorah in the window.

Or the doorway. Or set it up outside. Make it visible to passersby to remind everyone of the Hanukkah miracle.

2. Don't read by the light of the menorah.

Let the Hanukkah lights be symbolic, not practical.

3. Do eat foods fried in oil.

In honor of the sacred oil that lasted eight days. Potato latkes and doughnuts are popular choices.

4. Don't blow out the candles.

Hanukkah lights will shine for at least half an hour. After that, let them burn down by themselves.

5. Do eat cheese.

To remember the cheese Judith fed Holophernes.

6. Don't do work while the Hanukkah candles are burning. (If you are a girl.)

In honor of Judith's brave deeds, women relax and do no work as long as the candles burn.

7. Do fill the menorah from right to left.

The same direction as in reading Hebrew.

8. Don't light it that way.

Light the candles left to right, the newest candle first.

Thank a Teacher

The tradition of giving gifts at Hanukkah began with teachers. In the 1600s, Jewish children in Eastern Europe brought *gelt*—money—from their parents to their teachers at Hanukkah. Sometimes their parents gave them a little extra to keep. Today's presents of chocolate *gelt* and beautifully wrapped packages grew out of this tradition.

"We open one present a night for eight nights. Last year, my parents gave me a box of crayons the first night, a pad of paper the second night, then a set of watercolors, some paint brushes, glitter glue, markers, and scissors for the next five nights, and on the last night, I got an easel."

"We put the presents out on the first night of Hanukkah, but we don't open them till the eighth night. By then, we think we've figured out what's in the packages, but we're not always right."

"Our presents aren't things you can wrap. We're giving promises. I promise to clean my sister's aquarium."

One Good Turn

THANK YOU FOR CONTRIBUTING

OR HELPING TO FIND IMPORTANT INFORMATION:

Michael Berkowicz and Bonnie Srolovitz of Presentations Gallery in Mount Vernon, New York; Chris Boulis of the University of Pennsylvania Museum of Archaeology and Anthropology; Carnegie Library of Pittsburgh staff; Al Feinberg and Melissa Mathews, NASA Office of Public Affairs; Rabbi Baruch Goodman of Chabad House, New Brunswick, New Jersey; Jeffrey Hoffman, Ph.D., NASA Astronaut; Rabbi Sara Perman of Congregation Emanu-El Israel in Greensburg, Pennsylvania; Leah Perl Shollar, Judaic staff, Yeshiva Schools of Pittsburgh, Pennsylvania; Susan Wolfe of Palo Alto, California, granddaughter of Samuel Goldfarb.

THANK YOU FOR YOUR INSIGHTFUL SUGGESTIONS:

Dr. Fred Bortz, author of science books for young readers, Monroeville, Pennsylvania; Professor Jerome A. Chanes, Stern and Barnard Colleges, New York City; Gary Dreiblatt, science coordinator at The Abraham Joshua Heschel School, New York City; Judith Herschlag Muffs, Judaica consultant, New York City; Rachel Jacoby Rosenfield, Jewish educator, Riverdale, New York; Professor Seth Schwartz, Jewish Theological Seminary of America, New York City.

THANK YOU TO:

The Board of Jewish Education of Greater New York for permission to reprint the lyrics to "My Dreidel."

DREIDEL PAGE-TURNERS:

Bell, Robbie, and Michael Cornelius. *Board and Table Games Round the World*. Cambridge University Press, 1988.

Dobrinsky, Herbert C. *A Treasury of Sephardic Laws and Customs*. Yeshiva University Press, 1986.

Goodman, Phillip. *The Hanukkah Anthology*. Jewish Publication Society of America, 1976.

Gould, D. W. *The Top: Universal Toy, Enduring Pastime*. Clarkson N. Potter, 1973.

Zion, Noam Sachs, and Barbara Spectre. *A Different Light: The Hanukkah Book of Celebration*. Pitspopany Press, 2000.